Bitcoin

(Everything you need to know)

By

KELVIN WANG DX

Text Copyright © [Kelvin Wang DX]

All rights reserved. No part of this guide may be reproduced in any form without permission in writing from the publisher except in the case of brief quotations embodied in critical articles or reviews.

Legal & Disclaimer

The information contained in this book and its contents is not designed to replace or take the place of any form of medical or professional advice; and is not meant to replace the need for independent medical, financial, legal or other professional advice or services, as may be required. The content and information in this book has been provided for educational and entertainment purposes only.

The content and information contained in this book has been compiled from sources deemed reliable, and it is accurate to the best of the Author's knowledge, information and belief. However, the Author cannot guarantee its accuracy and validity and cannot be held liable for any errors and/or omissions. Further, changes are periodically made to this book as and when needed. Where appropriate and/or necessary, you must consult a professional (including but not limited to your doctor, attorney, financial advisor or such other professional advisor) before using any of the suggested remedies, techniques, or information in this book.

Upon using the contents and information contained in this book, you agree to hold harmless the Author from and against any damages, costs, and expenses, including any legal fees potentially resulting from the application of any of the information provided by this book. This disclaimer applies to any loss, damages or injury caused by the use and application, whether directly or indirectly, of any advice or information presented, whether for breach of contract, tort, negligence, personal injury, criminal intent, or under any other cause of action.

You agree to accept all risks of using the information presented inside this book.

You agree that by continuing to read this book, where appropriate and/or necessary, you shall consult a professional (including but not limited to your doctor, attorney, or financial advisor or such other advisor as needed) before using any of the suggested remedies, techniques, or information in this book.

Table of Contents

Introduction to Bitcoin: What is it? (And is not) 5
1. History of Bitcoin and its Origins 5
2. How are Bitcoins created? What is Bitcoin mining? 6
3. Clarifying some misconceptions about Bitcoin 6
4. Placing the value in Bitcoin 7
5. What Bitcoin is: 7
   1. Decentralized 7
   2. Open source 8
   3. Public asset ledger 9

Chapter 1: The Technology of Bitcoin. How do Bitcoins work? 10
1. The Centralized Database 10
2. Making Bitcoin transactions 11
3. Blockchain technology behind Bitcoin: The Distributed Database 11
4. Bitcoin Wallets 12

Chapter 2: How different is Bitcoin from regular currency? 13
1. Medium of exchange 13
2. Bitcoin's volatility 14
3. Pros to Bitcoins 15
   - Security 15
   - Lower fees 15
   - Instantaneous transactions 15
   - Not only limited to currency 15
   - Anonymity 15
4. Cons to Bitcoins 16
   - Too 'daunting' for ordinary users 16
   - No credit 16
   - Volatility 16

Chapter 3: Bitcoin in business 17
1. Money transfer 17
2. Exchanges 18
3. Web wallets 18
4. Mining 19
5. ATMs 19

Chapter 4: Should I invest in Bitcoin? 21
1. Dive in? 21

2. Stay Away? 21

Conclusion: What is the future of Bitcoin? 22

Also, Check Out This Other Book Published by Kelvin Wang DX 23

Free Preview Bonus 23

Introduction 24

CHAPTER 1: Reasons for Getting Into an Online 25

Business 25

    Goodbye to Traffic and Early Morning Rush 25
    No Need Putting Up with a Toxic Boss 25
    Working at your own Pace and Time 25
    Unlimited Income Potential 26
    Minimal Expenses for an Office 26
    Bigger Chance to Achieve more for Less Work 26
    Common Problems you will Encounter at the Start of your Online Business 27
        Tempting Opportunities and Resources 27
        Neglecting New Opportunities 27
        Doing Everything by Yourself 27
        Having Too Many Choices 27
        The Internet is Bigger than What You Think 28
        No Support from Family and Friend 28

Introduction to Bitcoin: What is it? (And is not)

When it comes to Bitcoin, the media coverage has not been shy about revealing to the public its existence and what it is. Indeed, several public figures have felt the pressure to at least talk about this openly and to also share their opinion about this new currency. Since Bitcoin is not a very simple concept, with it encompassing not only economics but brilliant software engineering as well and interestingly also intriguing cryptography. It is not surprising that people who comment their opinions about Bitcoin may not have a firmer grasp of how the technology works and the implications it holds. It is, therefore, this book's goal to provide you readers with the all the basics about Bitcoin that will eventually equip you with the necessary background information that allows you to reliably evaluate the worthiness of this innovative technology.

To be put in its simplest context, Bitcoin is nothing more but a computer program. This means that unlike real currency there is no one person or institution or possibly group of institutions/ persons controlling it. Unlike real currency, it also is not based or dependent on any physical merchandise such as gold. But these description about a digital currency seems close to impossible. If it is a computer program, surely someone controls it and more so created it. Thus, we start by first understanding how Bitcoin came to be.

1. History of Bitcoin and its Origins

Bitcoin, indeed, has a creator (or a group of creators), however, his or her identity has been kept private during the entire process of releasing Bitcoin. Except for a pseudonym, no one else knew about the mastermind to the whole ingenious technology. The person used the name Satoshi Nakamoto and he or she intended the technology as an open source software, so in a sense no one and everyone owns the code. Bitcoin is owned by the public domain and thus no one technically owns and controls it.

The first time the world has ever heard of Bitcoin was in November 2008, when Satoshi Nakamoto – again, just an anonymous pseudo name – posted a cryptography mailing list entitled "*Bitcoin: A Peer-to-Peer Electronic Cash System.*" It was only a couple months after until the Bitcoin network was finally running and has started accommodating its first open source client and the use of the first ever Bitcoins in the history of mankind. Of course, spearheaded by Satoshi Nakamoto, he was named the first block of Bitcoin mined as the "genesis block" and was worth a reward of 50 Bitcoins.

Given that it is a complex software, it also makes sense that the initial transactions would be among fellow software and computer experts. So, on the day when the technology was released, the first ever supporters and contributors to Bitcoin is also a programmer named Hal Finney, who received the first Bitcoin transfer of 10 Bitcoins from Satoshi Nakamoto himself in what appears to be the first ever Bitcoin transaction. Transaction that has marked a revolutionary technology.

2. How are Bitcoins created? What is Bitcoin mining?

Bitcoins are created by a method called Bitcoin mining, and no it does not mean picking up an pick, going underground and painstakingly digging for a physical representation of monetary value. Remember, we are talking about digital currency and as such mining involves a digital acquisition of the currency. Bitcoin mining is the competitive and decentralized process of generating Bitcoins. This procedure comprises the compensation of individuals by the network as a reward for their services. People who earn Bitcoins, individuals we call Bitcoin miners, are those who would process businesses and secure the network using dedicated hardware and in return these people get rewarded in Bitcoins for their services.

The way mining for Bitcoin works is that it allows for new Bitcoins to be created but only at a fixed rate. This means that the value of the Bitcoin remains at a set level for a given period. This property of Bitcoin and how it is being created creates a highly competitive environment for Bitcoin mining. As more and more miners join the throng of mining, the competition gets tighter and tougher and it becomes progressively difficult to earn a profit through mining. With the increase in demand for transactions and jobs, miners must respond by increasing their efficiency. One way to improve efficiency is by cutting on expenses which are related to the operation of the business transaction. There is no central authority that would dictate and manipulate the system so that they end up earning more profits. Each miner gets equal footing, the only difference is the amount of mining job you are willing to take in. And the network ensures the fidelity of this process is kept by making certain that every Bitcoin node in any corner of the world would reject any transaction that does not observe the rules built for the network and are expected of every miner to comply with.

The creation of these Bitcoins is consistently decreasing and at a predictable rate. New Bitcoin production is automatically reduced in half every year and over time until eventually the creation of bitcoins would stop completely upon reaching a total number of 21 million Bitcoins. Much of the earnings that Bitcoin miners receive are almost exclusively out of the numerous small transaction fees.

3. Clarifying some misconceptions about Bitcoin

First and foremost, since Bitcoin is a decentralized digital currency there is no single person or even an institution that manage or controls it. It is decentralized, and more about Bitcoin's decentralized nature will be explained in the middle of this chapter. Bitcoin also, unlike common currencies (or other would argue, like some common currencies) is not backed by any physical good such as precious metals or gems, gold or silver. It is not a physical currency but instead is just a free source computer algorithm that is free for anyone to download, use at their own means and modify in whatever manner they want it to fit to their purpose.

One very controversial myth about Bitcoin is that it is a Ponzi scheme, about the infamous Italian swindler and con artist Charles Ponzi in the early 1920s. NO, Bitcoin is not some elaborate form of fraud where there is a central person who facilitates operations of paying revenues to present investors from money invested in later or upcoming investors. Foremost to this argument is the fact that, as we've previously mentioned, there is no one person managing Bitcoin, thus there is no one person who could profit from such a scheme should it exist in Bitcoin technology. Secondly, there is no means by which revenues can be deflected to pay off old transactions from new transactions. Transfers of the bitcoin currency is solely managed by the users and they can initiate these transfers at their own will, the Bitcoin technology has no control whatsoever at these transactions so there is no way it can facilitate deflection of funds. Thirdly, a new investment in the Bitcoin network is equivalent to an equal disinvestment. Investors in Bitcoin usually use the currency as means of exchange where they would purchase the bitcoin from another user who is selling it. This means there is no new investment, just exchange. The amount linked into a bitcoin matches the amount that has flown out of it.

4. Placing the value in Bitcoin

The primary reason why bitcoins would have value rests in the fact that they are useful as certain form of money. The bitcoin currency has all the properties normal money would have. It is long-lasting, it can be transferred, it can be interchanged or exchanged, it protects its value by being limited, it can be split and very recently it is an identifiable form of currency. But rather than relying on the physical property of money (value in precious metals or gold or silver) or trust in central governance, bitcoin relies on its ability to be divided, multiplied, subtracted on and added upon. With all these qualities, all it really takes is trust from the society and its acceptance and implementation in the community and bitcoin now has value. As a point of fact, Bitcoin has already increased its value as more and more users are patronizing it and many more starting businesses are preferring it over conventional money. Just like all the money we are using worldwide, the value has its intimate relationship with the willingness of people to use it and associate significance to it.

5. What Bitcoin is:

1. Decentralized

This is quite possibly the most innovative feature of Bitcoin – it is decentralized. This means that there is no central server that operates the procedures of Bitcoin. How Bitcoin works is that it functions through a peer-to-peer network of computers that have been linked together. Bitcoin technology is the pioneer in its field, meaning it is the first ever digital currency that have been built in a decentralized way.

Most of the sovereign currencies we use today are sanctioned currencies where the currency is usually released by the government and its dispense is managed by a central bank. Like all the other currencies or money in the world, the common currencies we use now don't have values in its own. It is all these social conventions and consensus values we link with money that provides its worth. So, in a sense, the currencies we use today are all "fiat" money where a government decree has issued it legal to use the note for monetary exchange. The acknowledgment of the currency's value all boils down to the acceptance of the masses. A currency can lose its value as soon as the confidence of the society to its policy and distribution is lost. If everyone else believes a hundred-dollar bill does not account for anything then it will lose its value and will be just that, a small rectangular piece of note with an image of Benjamin Franklin.

2. Open source

When we talk about open source software, this means that the source code – or the text listing all the set of commands compiled and assembled to make up an executable computer program – is available for anyone to download, copy, use, modify and redistribute however the user sees fit. In the computer and mobile device era and the age of the internet, each of us has had at least one experience operating and using an open source software product. An excellent example would be the internet website browser you are using to surf the internet such as Google Chrome, Firefox and Internet Explorer. If you are not too familiar with computers then you may have at least been acquainted with mobile devices such as a cellular phone or tablet. These gadgets operate under free software such as Android or iOS. In fact, a huge portion of devices we use now runs on open source software, we might not just be too aware about their existence. It has been the goal of programmers who develop these source codes to make the development and sharing of these programs as open as possible. To them, it is their academic and intellectual duty to society to not make profit out of their developed codes. This can be likened to peer-reviewed publications in the scientific research community. By creating transparency in the codes that programmers develop, open source allows for the increase in the quality of the software.

The distinctive line that separates open source software from proprietary software is the licenses that this software has. For proprietary software, its license allows users to copy and use the software under the agreement that the ownership of the software remains with the programmer who published it. On the other hand, open source software licenses would grant the user to use, copy, modify and redistribute the software with the copyright of the software remaining to with the publisher of the program but the license transfers the rights to the user as well, under certain obligations specifically stated in the license.

Bitcoin, since it has been released as an open source software, now has a life of its own as soon as it was made available to the public. The issuer does not have to constantly maintain and update it since other developers now have taken over to control it in their own specific use. Therefore, it does not really matter for the Bitcoin technology who Satoshi Nakamoto is or if he is still actively managing his software, because as far as the open source code platform is concerned, Bitcoin will continue to prosper so long as there is one interested party for the program.

3. Public asset ledger

Central to the operations of the Bitcoin network is a circulated database that holds a copy of the mutual asset ledger. Since this database is being circulated and disseminated, each participant in the entire network, which would represent a node, gets to have a copy of this ledger. Copies of this ledger that are being held by each node are coherent and similar by design.

Given that there is a public asset ledger does not mean that the user loses control of his or her own funds, instead the user gets to manage his or her own funds by using a cryptographic private key. Whenever a user wants to spend some more funds, the user must use this key that would enable her to sign a message indicating the receiver of the funds and the amount the user wishes to send. It is then that the user would broadcast this transaction by sharing the signed message to the network, and then every user of the Bitcoin network receives a copy of the message. With this transparency, each node holds the opportunity to authenticate and validate the message and update its internal database appropriately.

Chapter 1: The Technology of Bitcoin. How do Bitcoins work?

Bitcoin is not the first technology that has enabled the digital transfer of money, in fact a lot of other corporations and companies have already been well established in the business of wiring money digitally. However, where Bitcoin sets an edge as a trailblazer in the digital money industry is that up until Bitcoin, the process of transmitting money has always been mediated by a third party. To perform transactions digitally, a third person needed to facilitate the process. Bitcoin sets the stage at allowing users to make digital payments without the need for these third-party mediators. How exactly does Bitcoin do this?

1. The Centralized Database

When it comes to creating, and utilizing digital money, the crucial part is assigning value to a certain data pattern which in the world of programming is the very basic and simple (yet can be incomprehensibly complex) binary digits 0's and 1's. The pitfall of only using these binary digits to represent a digital value is that this can very easily be replicated. For instance, one can very easily copy and send the same binary numbers representing a certain value to anyone. Therefore, for digital money to be effective and functioning, there needs to be a system where accountability to each money is afforded. The solution to this is the creation of a central database that would hold a list of all users and the funds that any one of them would hold.

It is in this way that we make sure each digital money (essentially the code) would be unique and scarce so that it does not lose its value. Also, vital to the success of this system is the religious updating and broadcasting of the transactions that take place in transferring these digital currencies, i.e. who holds what at some certain point in time.

The caveat to this centralized database is, although advertised as open source, any person who wants to use bitcoin must have previously registered with the central database to operate.

More importantly, the major issue that could possibly arise for running a centralized database is that if an attacker would want to ruin the system, once he gets hold of the central database, he or she could just as easily tamper with the ownership of any funds. Even scarier is the thought that in the wrong hands, the centralized database is very vulnerable in that a simple system shutdown of the centralized database server could result to a loss of very vital (and expensive) information.

2. Making Bitcoin transactions

Users of bitcoins would each have a unique identifier assigned to them which are just long combinations of letters and numbers. These "usernames" are then stored in the Bitcoin network public ledger that links the bitcoins associated with the account. Each user would now have a public-private cryptographic key where the public part of the key is the address of the user and the private part would be solely for the user's knowledge and use.

To send a bitcoin to another user, the sending user must use the private key to sign a message that indicates the desire to transfer a certain amount of money to a second user. The sender does not have to identify who he or she wants to send the funds to, the only information needed is the address of that receiver. As nodes within the Bitcoin network – all the other users of the Bitcoin technology – receives the message for the transaction, they will have to verify that the message is correct. It is at this point that users can reject the message if they think there is something wrong with it. Users also get to check if the sender has sufficient funds for the transaction, transaction is deemed invalid if there are insufficient funds. Then finally, other users update the database where funds get transferred from one address to another.

It is important to note here that the other users need not know the identities of either party for the transaction because all they needed to know are the sender's and receiver's address. These public addresses are generated by that user's device used for the transaction and to enhance privacy of the user, he or she can generate as much addresses as possible.

Bitcoin transactions are very straightforward and simple and there need not be any prior registration for inexperienced users to use Bitcoin. A new user can even create a communication about an impending Bitcoin transaction by sharing their addresses through text messages, chat, email or pairing of two smartphones. Then a Bitcoin transaction can be initiated and the network will accept the transaction (given everything else is valid) even though it has never seen the newly generated address before.

3. Blockchain technology behind Bitcoin: The Distributed Database

The public database that users keep in the Bitcoin network is called the *blockchain*. The transactions are clustered in blocks of transactions every specified amount of time, approximately 10 minutes. Then these transactions are recorded one after another in a chain of blocks, and that is how they got the name blockchain.

This format was specially designed to prevent any form of hacking to take place. Since each block is linked to generate a record of the past transactions and this record cannot be tampered upon or altered. The link between blocks is a cryptographic link that cannot be easily duplicated and hacked, given the impressive amount of the data that the user needs to hack.

The way Bitcoin attains unanimity in its distributed database is by creating these massive amounts of computational power that ensures users continue to secure the network from attack. A user lending his or her computational power will, in return, be compensated with new bitcoins for ensuring the integrity of the blockchain.

4. Bitcoin Wallets

Just as how real-life wallets contain the money of a person, the software that enables users to organize his or her bitcoins is called a wallet. This software holds the user's private key or keys. It is through wallets that users can create transactions they wish to send through the network and this is where the user can perform the transactions that will then allow him or her to monitor the funds left in his or her account. Wallets also enable users to manage through all the different addresses linked to the users account. Wallets also enables the user to generate new addresses he or she can use during transactions and allows users to sing the transaction using the private key.

Wallets therefore keep the private key, and since without this private key the user can no longer authorize any transaction (the user still has the funds and they are kept in the distributed ledger, the user just won't be able to sign any transaction), the loss of a private key could very well mean the loss of the funds as well. It is for this reason that it is highly recommended that users keep backups of their private keys. These wallets are very important in creating and keeping these backups for the users.

With all these being said, you probably know how important these wallets are by now, mostly because it keeps information about the user's private key. If another person gets hold of the private key, the other person can just as easily send all the funds to another address that she has control over. It is therefore crucially important that users properly secure the private keys they have in their wallets, especially upon using the internet. Many wallets are associated with the encryption technology that allows the user to secure the private key, where he or she must input a generated password to be able to use the private key. This may be slightly inconvenient for the user because he or she needs to input a password every time a transaction is being made. But what little price to pay to ensure that your account does not get compromised.

Chapter 2: How different is Bitcoin from regular currency?

Currently there are about 180 currencies that are being circulated and used around the world, at least the ones that are legally recognized by the United Nations. Although many historians and scholars would argue that the first instance of humans using a formal form of money dates as far back as a thousand decades (or more) ago, way back before human prehistory, in record and in the books, the British pound holds the record for being the world's oldest currency that is still being used today. The British pound was recorded to be used as early as the 8th century and until today the British continue to make use of this currency.

But what is money exactly? It appears that it's nothing more bit a token or symbol that societies developed to perform uninformed and more efficient trade. Barter system has been around within human communities as early as the 10th millennium BC, and it was almost inevitable for humans to develop a form of recognized trade. So now instead of having to exchange live cattle or bags of grain for a yard full of scarf, we get to enjoy the benefits and convenience that current currency affords us.

In its simplest core, Bitcoin could also serve as money as it also fulfills the simplest technical attributes of money. First, bitcoin is durable in a sense that it provides stability and that long-lasting property common money have. Like money we use now, we can do all sorts of math with bitcoin as well, we can add it up, subtract from it, divide it and even multiply its value. Bitcoin is mutually interchangeable in that you can barter and purchase goods with it. Bitcoin is easily transferable, in fact one of the advantages and appeals of bitcoin is its mobility and ease of transport and use. And finally, and possibly what most central banks are putting much effort in maintaining their currencies into, bitcoin is almost impossible to counterfeit.

However, there has still been a lot of heated debate whether bitcoin should be considered a currency or not. Faultfinders might criticize that bitcoin does not seem to fulfill the main functions of conventional money. First off, it is not even tangible! But supporters of the Bitcoin technology would heavily argue that an asset does not have to be tangible to be valuable.

In this chapter, we shall talk about the properties of bitcoin that reflects its role in economics and how it may, or may not be, like conventional currency.

1. Medium of exchange

As of date, tens of thousands are now patronizing bitcoin and are using it to conduct their businesses. With this information, there appears to be an obvious practical data that would support the idea that bitcoin can serve as a medium of exchange. Since its introduction into society, there seems to be a steady increase in the number of transactions utilizing bitcoin in their business. There are close to a hundred thousand transactions in the Bitcoin network per day, and although this is still considerably lower than other conventional currencies it has been used as a medium of exchange.

Traditional economists may say that for it to be recognized as a universal medium of exchange, the number of users must continue to expand and increase. But it appears that Bitcoin only needs to continue improving and expanding its network and it'll only be a few years until it can finally reach its critical mass point, or that instance where the benefits to the inexperienced users will exceed the cost of having to adapt to the innovative technology. In other words, to be considered a universal medium of exchange, Bitcoin should be used by at least a steady number of users so that for performing transactions, users wouldn't have to resort to other currencies because bitcoin affords them the convenience and efficiency.

2. Bitcoin's volatility

Possibly the biggest concern critics and supporters alike would have of Bitcoin technology is its volatility or its liability to change rapidly and unpredictably. Since 2011, Bitcoin's value has spiked up to 1200 its initial value by the start of 2014 only to dip a sharp decrease a couple months after, and today it plays around the 1000 value mark, the value continues to be very volatile. With this property, it is not surprising for economists and investors and money enthusiasts to consider the technology as a highly risky investment than as a stable store of value.

This unpredictable nature of bitcoin is often likened to the dynamics of a start-up business. Bitcoin is indeed increasing in value, however its speed of being utilized as a primary medium of exchange is not as competitive as conventional currencies or digital currencies for that matter. This low turnover of Bitcoin is because a lot of users who are diving into the Bitcoin network are holding on to their bitcoins as an investment instead of using it in circulation as a medium of exchange. In fact, Bitcoin has been associated with such high values that most bitcoins are now being held and kept under stagnant accounts. This phenomenon has been termed the *hoarding* of bitcoins.

A currency's property to function as a medium of exchange and as an item to be used with higher purchasing value in the future are complementary properties. No one would resort to the currency if they do not have value, on the one hand if they had too much value no one would want to keep using and circulating them for fear of missing out on probable future investments. The Bitcoin network, namely the users patronizing the technology, should have to balance these two functions to allow bitcoin to grow as a currency. They would have to know when they need to hold on to their bitcoins, and they should also be wise enough to know when they should let it go and allow it to circulate in the network. If the hoarding of bitcoins continues and possibly worsen, it is not hard to imagine that people would recognize it as a currency to scarce and hard to grab a hold of that bitcoin would soon lose its purpose as a medium of exchange.

3. Pros to Bitcoins

- ### Security

Quite possibly, bitcoin's biggest appeal to users is its close to nothing security breaches. If someone tries to hack a bank or robs a business, the moment the robber gets a hold of the safe or cash register then that day's profits could be considered down the drain. In contrast, since Bitcoin does not use any tangible currency should an attacker get a hold of a user's private keys, that attacker does not really gain any value since the original user would always have control over the private keys. Critics of Bitcoin would point out that these wallets and transactions are not entirely safe from security breaches. Maybe due to its young nature in the business, no massive hack has still ever been reported but should one ever occur then there would be no remedy for the users.

- ### Lower fees

On average, credit card fees would be from 5-30% of the transaction, in comparison bitcoin transactions are lower than these. However, critics might argue that if you try adding costs for theft protection and other regulatory costs the final added cost for the transaction could be comparable to these fees.

- ### Instantaneous transactions

Compared to conventional bank transfers or wire transfers and remittances that would normally take days to weeks for it to finally be settled and completed, bitcoin transactions are fulfilled almost instantaneously. But still, modern technology of money transfers and transactions, especially the use of online tools and smartphone apps, are all working better to also offer this close to real-time exchange of money.

- ### Not only limited to currency

Since Bitcoin does not limit itself to only currency and you can basically take advantage of the open source code to transact the business, transfers are not only limited to money transfers but to other digital assets as well. This innovation opens a door of unlimited possibilities such as exchange of other contracts or specific applications to the users.

- ## Anonymity

When performing transactions in the Bitcoin network, users can keep their identity anonymous by using pseudonyms or only using decrypted information about their identity. On the other end of the spectrum, transactions can also be performed with decreased privacy so that the users do not fall prey to the attack of hackers that are trying to access the complete financial information of the user by determining the address of the user.

4. Cons to Bitcoins

- ### Too 'daunting' for ordinary users

Since Bitcoin technology prides itself with its complex blockchain backbone, many people who barely knows anything about programming and more so about the economics of money exchange might get easily intimidated by the technology. As a result, users might have to resort to the use of intermediaries that will be paid just for the sole purpose of making Bitcoin transactions clear to the clients. So, this might defeat the purpose of decreasing costs in the transactions. At some point, it may even be more of a burden than a convenience.

- ### No credit

The United States of America, and most of the developed countries of the world, runs and functions under credits and credit scores. Unfortunately, Bitcoin still does not offer this credit option to its clients. Supporters, however, argue that this option could easily be incorporated into their transactions, users just must tailor fit this service into their system.

- ### Volatility

Fiat currencies are managed by central banks and there are authorities making sure that the value continues to be stable. Bitcoin does not have this form of backup. Thus, the price and value of bitcoin is heavily in mercy of its users and transactions, which could be an advantage on itself but the moment things get downhill and a huge crack is made within the system, this could mean a massive blow to the stability of the system. As such, this appears to be the most vulnerable aspect of Bitcoin.

Chapter 3: Bitcoin in business

Bitcoin has been created primarily to address the costs of conducting payment transactions. Here in this chapter we shall look at some of the first round of and most common business applications of bitcoin.

Since this is a recent form of technology, we still haven't begun to see the wide range of applications that Bitcoin technology could be applied into. We are still scratching at the surface of the endless possibilities of Bitcoin use but the list in this chapter will showcase the dynamics bitcoin has provided into the mode of transaction for these businesses.

1. Money transfer

The World Bank averages the money transfer fees in remittance centers or companies in the range of about 10%. In contrast, common Bitcoin transactions are only 0.01% to 0.05%, a huge slash by about a hundred from the average transfer fee we pay in transaction fees! Theoretically, Bitcoin has the advantage when it comes to cost of money transfer, but there are some reasons as to why this cost advantage may also be restricted for Bitcoin users.

Much of the costs for money transmittance goes into the administrative and regulatory costs of the transaction. The clients get to pay for these costs. It is presumed that as bitcoin gets larger and the startup business patronizing it gets more successful with larger clientele, then the business will have to eventually start charging their clients as well just to keep the business going.

One other caveat of money transfer is the availability of the right kind of technology that allows for Bitcoin transactions. Not all countries may have the same technological advancement that would make Bitcoin convenient, so this limits the client pool for money transfer and possibly to compensate for this disadvantage the Bitcoin transmitter may have to pay more just to accommodate cases for these countries.

Conversely, the limitation for technology could also transcend to limitation in the liquidity of Bitcoin to the local fiat currency. This would greatly increase money transfer cost just because very little converters recognize Bitcoin.

Still, supporters could see the potential of Bitcoin in the money transfer business. Especially considering the public ledger that creates transparency in the transaction where small businesses don't have to be heavily invested in their own personal means of creating security since Bitcoin already did that for them.

Utilizing Bitcoin in the massive remittance market is still a hot area of discussion, especially since its sustainability is still uncertain.

2. Exchanges

The exchanges, like foreign exchange markets, allows for the conversion of bitcoins into fiat money. Foreign exchanges, especially for the major currencies of the world such as US dollars, British pounds, and Japanese yen, are highly dynamic. Changing values almost every second.

The way these exchanges occurs is usually via a third-party model where a user would deposit their funds under a certain currency, an exchange is initiated and processed to account for the other denomination's value. The funds are kept in the user's account and only when the user orders for a withdrawal of the funds do they finally leave the exchange.

The way to make these exchanges using bitcoins is to also deposit the fund into a third-party model, thus leaving the blockchain recording system. The widespread practice of Bitcoin users is to keep the funds in the storage and only allow a certain small proportion of their funds in the wallets so that they would have direct control over it. Exchanges using bitcoin can be done by signing arbitrary messages using the private keys and transferring these funds from one address to another.

3. Web wallets

This system is a different system than the Bitcoin wallet, in fact this business is profiting by masking all the complexities of managing Bitcoin wallets for first-time users to utilize the technology without being daunted by its complexities. The way it works is quite like how online banking would work. Users would be requested to create an account online and deposit their bitcoins with the web wallet service. All payments and transactions would then be performed via the Web Wallet provider's platform and website. This convenience is not the only advantage web wallets provide their users. Web wallets also, like online banks, alert a user whenever there is a breach in the security of his or her wallet. Through their record tracking, web wallets could also warn a user in an event that the user is about to transact with another user with poor reputation. Web wallet services could protect their clients from possibly transferring bitcoins to bogus addresses intended to mislead users. Web wallets also allows users to link their accounts to their bank accounts.

As you can see there are a lot of risks for these services as well, most important of these is trusting all your information to new businesses (given the newness of Bitcoin technology) that are of higher risk of security breach. They are of course of higher risk since they are prized targets from attackers. Users must be very wary of putting all their eggs in one basket, and most especially wary of the web wallet service providers that they are choosing.

4. Mining

As already mentioned early on the previous chapter, miners would be able to generate revenues by the *block rewards* system on top of the transaction fees that they can collect off other users. If there are for instance about 20 bitcoins per block, the total mining revenue could reach up to 1 million bitcoins and if each bitcoin is about 500 USD, the annual revenue for the Bitcoin mining industry would be roughly 500 million US dollars! This, without question, is currently one of the biggest businesses that operates under the Bitcoin network.

Bitcoin mining industry is any type of business that would secure the proper and secure functioning of the Bitcoin network. Different business models that are under this big Bitcoin industry includes the equipment manufacturers, such as companies that would design and distribute the actual hardware for Bitcoin technology. The developers of processors and the chip manufacturers. They all benefit greatly as the Bitcoin industry continues to expand. As final equipment gets produced by the manufacturers, data centers then start hosting this equipment. Datacenters also profit from Bitcoin mining. The people who run the mining hardware- the Bitcoin miners – directly profit from this business and earning from block rewards. Directly managing these miners are mining pool operators who function as managers that allows for the smooth transactions of rewards to miners. The Bitcoin mining has indeed improved greatly that more specific positions and equipment are being utilized to keep this industry going.

5. ATMs

Automated Teller Machines for Bitcoin functions like conventional ATMs but instead of dispensing cash it functions the other way around where users can buy or sell bitcoins with cash. The procedure of operating a Bitcoin ATM pretty much follows the following steps:

1. User scans her ID and waits for the ATM to verify it.

2. User inputs cash and presents ATM with a QR code (usually generated by a Bitcoin wallet online or on a smartphone) that holds information about the user's public address.

3. ATM sends the purchased bitcoins into the directed address.

The way these ATMs profits is through the operation fee which is usually within the 3% – 7% range. Early users of Bitcoin ATMs were usually the curious users who were simply intrigued with the technology but now supporters have seen its value for travelers who could carry the bitcoins anywhere they go and simply exchange it to local currency in their destination country.

Chapter 4: Should I invest in Bitcoin?

1. Dive in?

From as little as less than a dollar in its conception in 2011, Bitcoins now reach up to 3800$ as we speak! So, if that 3799$ increase is not enough motivation to entice you to get into the business of investing in bitcoins, then you may just be the person who's not into investing altogether. Bitcoin is indeed a highly appealing concept and technology and since there will only ever be 21 million of these coins to be created, as production stops the chances of the value continuing to increase is very likely, especially if the demands for this currency remains increasing at the rate as it is now experiencing.

2. Stay Away?

While there have certainly been a lot of people who have made a lot of money by owning bitcoins, a lot of critics have been reading at its value and taking its advantages with a huge grain of salt. After all, the close to two decades of the Bitcoin network's history has shown how extremely unpredictable the system is. The prices fluctuate a lot and conventional investors are put off by this idea of high volatility and extremely considerable risk. However, as is true with pretty much all investments these are nothing more but speculations and the only best way to answer this is to wait for time to tell for certain.

Conclusion: What is the future of Bitcoin?

To date, Bitcoin has recently reached its $5000 mark! A lot of the investment players and money enthusiasts have high hopes for the future of Bitcoin, especially since it has been a resounding topic of discussion in the mainstream now. Like gold, the value is not controlled by any authority and its value solely rests in the value users and enthusiasts would account to it. And since a lot of investors are dead serious about the possibility of Bitcoin, there may be little chance of it going extinct in the market, at least soon. What makes Bitcoin even more valuable is the fact that only 21 million Bitcoins will ever be released and the deadline for Bitcoin production is fast approaching. After 2140, no new Bitcoins will ever be supplied for the public and this gives Bitcoin more and more value.

On the one hand, users should also be cautious as they surely tread on thin ice as they venture into Bitcoin technology. First, Bitcoin is a digital currency founded on crypto technology and are vulnerable to security breach, but then again so is every high-end bank where we keep our money nowadays. Also, Bitcoin is very volatile and increases the risk to its users.

So, the bottom line when it comes to utilizing the Bitcoin technology and joining in the Bitcoin network is to always (ALWAYS!) exercise caution. Only commit to what you can afford to lose and never pour in all you have for something that is not too sure. Remember, you only reserve regrets once it's too late.

Also, Check Out This Other Book Published by Kelvin Wang DX

e-Business Blueprint

Free Preview Bonus

Introduction

With an economic whiplash that hits most of the countries today; more people are joining ranks in achieving economic progress through the internet. The internet world had become an American Dream while others look at it as the other side of the world with the greener pasture.

Many had indeed taken their chance in starting an online business, yet not all are ready to face all the challenges and the complexities of surviving in the internet business arena.

However, for those who were lucky enough to survive, they lived to testify to the kind of life online business offers.

This eBook, "e-Business Blueprint: Your Pass to Financial Freedom" aims to provide beginners with a guide on setting up an online business and guiding you through the simple steps to achieve success.

With proper knowledge and determination, success on any online business can be achievable and in fact, rewarding. It's just a matter of planning and driving your towards a goal that can really make your dream comes true.

CHAPTER 1: Reasons for Getting Into an Online Business

People got various reasons for going into online business. But most often, online business is for people who got tired of working 8-5 or 9-6 every day. Rushing each morning for a gulp of coffee before fighting his way through traffic and hoping he could be earlier than usual!

As you realized that you are getting tired of working for someone else and you want to become your own boss, you start thinking of the possibility to make it big in the internet business. Hoping, you are right, and then the best way to set up a business with a greater chance to make it to success is to start now!

Here are just a few of the many reasons why you should start with your internet business.

Goodbye to Traffic and Early Morning Rush

With an internet business, you don't need to rush up too early that you need to skip eating breakfast just so you can arrive in time for work. But when you are living in an overcrowded metropolis where you had to go through jam-packed traffic, stress and anxiety can be a daily part of your routine!

Online business can help you save a lot of money by not traveling every day. Count the savings you can have when you don't need to go out for work. You can likewise save your time and convert the time spent for daily trips into more productive inputs.

No Need Putting Up with a Toxic Boss

Most often people got fed up and want to get out of their work because they have a toxic person for a boss. Most often, bosses thought that their employees are there to please them all the time. This often happens when you are working in a sole proprietorship type of business or a one-man organization. Most often than not, you feed to your boss whims and schemes rather than get productive in your tasks. In the end, you feel thoroughly burnt out and find a quick way to change job.

Working at your own Pace and Time

When you are running an online business, you can be your own boss. You can work at a chosen time and place. You can even have more time to yourself and to your family. However, this can have its own drawback. So, before you get out of your work, be sure your finances or the lack of will not cripple you. Proper timing is needed so your family will not suffer from your decision.

When you are free to decide for yourself whether you are going to work or not, be sure you manage your time effectively and efficiently. When you're alone to manage your time and no one is around to put pressure on you, you don't give yourself a reason to procrastinate. You need to learn to balance everything even without someone to answer to. Remember that every minute wasted is an opportunity lost in online business.

Unlimited Income Potential

Working on a regular career means putting up a cap on how much you can earn. But with online business, your ability to earn depends on how much time you want to put into your business. You can earn as much or as little as you want. The market for online business is too vast. You just learn to tap its unlimited resources and you go as far as you can.

You can target people around the world as the global market is getting bigger and bigger and more people are learning how to access the internet every day. You can work as much or as little as you choose. The marketplace for internet businesses is worldwide.

According to the later report of the Statistics portal, the number of internet users had risen up to 3.17 billion this year from 2.94 of the previous year. Isn't that market large enough to dip your toes into?

Minimal Expenses for an Office

Since you are working from the comfort of your home, you don't need to rent an office space. You will again be saving a lot on your administrative expenses compared if you are running a conventional type of business.

In setting up your business, all you need to have is your laptop or PC and low-cost hardware and software which you can even get for free online if you're just diligent enough to browse through your internet.

Bigger Chance to Achieve more for Less Work

An online business allows you to work fewer hours and achieve more. There are some business models that can be fully automated. You just have to set them up and (lo!), they can run on their own and earns you a passive income. This automation process now is widely used in the internet market. If you can't run your business on 100% automation, you can at least have it automated at 50% or more, so you can have more time for additional business to carry on.

What makes an online business unique than conventional ones is you can operate multiple businesses single-handedly. To simplify, you are operating a business that is almost next to impossible – Less capital, less time, and less effort for unlimited income streams potentials.

Common Problems you will Encounter at the Start of your Online Business

Starting your online business can be both rewarding and stimulating. However, you are sure to encounter a few problems that new entrepreneurs usually encounter. To steer clear of these issues, you must be aware of them and avoid them as they come along.

Tempting Opportunities and Resources

As you start hanging on the internet, you will be meeting a lot of opportunities along with remarkable resources to promising you great support in your online business. These products, usually software or a business opportunity, may be as great as their vendor advertise them. Nonetheless, if you jump from one opportunity to another, you will be losing your focus on your core business. It is, therefore, important that you start an online business with only what you absolutely need and have it run smoothly before getting into another. The same works with your software or any other tool.

Neglecting New Opportunities

Basically, this is the exact opposite of grabbing every opportunity that comes along. If you refuse to examine or look at any new opportunity sent your way because you have your focus set up trying to achieve a goal with a method that simply don't work, avoid overlooking the warning signs that tell you that you need to move on or move in another direction.

Doing Everything by Yourself

When you think it's better to keep all the profit, you keep trying to do everything so you can keep the money to yourself. Saving is always good for your business, but as your business develops, it will become impossible for you to embrace all the tasks. This is the time when you need to develop some way to ease up your workload. An example of these if subscribing for an auto responder that will take care of your mailing activities. Instead of manually sending letters, answering queries, the auto-responder allows you to maintain and develop relationships with your customer base and up-sell or cross-sell your products and services.

Having Too Many Choices

Affiliate marketing is a good start for an online business for you can earn as soon as someone buys from your inks. This is the reason why it is so popular with many people. Affiliate marketing method has many positive aspects but there are too many choices that it is confusing to know which to promote. Before you jump into marketing a new software by way of an affiliate program, check how much commission you can earn from it, how you can get paid, and know if there is some support you can get from the owner. It is also important to know if the product sells before promoting it.

The Internet is Bigger than What You Think

Having an online business doesn't mean that people will naturally visit your website and buy things that you offer. The internet is such an enormous marketplace that you need to know how to get prospective customers to visit your visit so you can have the chance to convert these visits into sales. Meaning, you need to learn how to generate website traffic by utilizing both free and paid traffic generators.

No Support from Family and Friend

Sometimes, we presume that our family and friends will be our loyal customer. Sad to say, in most cases, it doesn't usually happen especially during the start of your business. There are even cases when they will discourage you from doing online business. Though these people mean well, don't get easily swayed and let your goals and efforts get destructed. If you have set your goal and created a business plan to back it up, you have every opportunity to get successful.

Regardless of whom you are, your age, gender, technical skills, educational background, you can always start your own internet business. You can always harness whatever skill you have through various learning platforms and resources provided on the internet for a certain fee or for free.

DOWNLOAD e-Business Blueprint NOW!